PHOTOGRAPHY 101

The Only Guide You Will Need

DISCLAIMER

TABLE OF CONTENTS

Exposing the Secrets of the Exposure Triangle

the Skinny on Shutter Speed

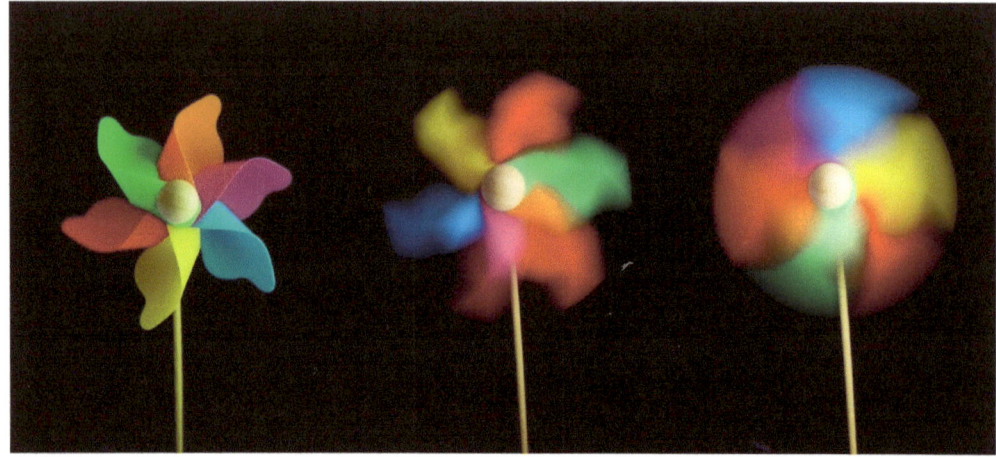

FIGURE 1. SHUTTER SPEED

In order to understand shutter speed, it is better that we also know what a shutter is and how it works. The shutter is the front part of a camera that stays shut until the camera is used to take a picture. As you begin to take a picture, the shutter will open and allow light inside. The rays will make their way to the exposed sensor via the aperture. The shutter will stay open until the light required has been collected, after which it will close to protect the sensor.

The speed at which the shutter will open or exposure time is also known as shutter speed. As long as the shutter stays open, the sensor will be exposed to light, which means the longer it stays open, the more light will hit the sensor. The shutter speed will vary between camera types. Since the opening and closing takes a short time, the unit of measurement for shutter speed is fractions of a second. In order to estimate how much light the camera's sensor is being exposed to, you can do this simple calculation:

¼ of a second will let in half the amount of light as ½ would.

Two things that you need to keep in mind when it comes to shutter speed are that it is related to both light and motion. That means, if you leave the shutter open for a longer period, and then the pictures will be brighter. However, if the shutter speed is fast, then the sensor will only be exposed to the light for a brief fraction of a second. Consequently, the pictures will turn out darker. How can you use this information to your advantage? If a picture looks dark, then retake it with a slower shutter speed and vice versa.

Regarding shutter speed's relationship to motion, it is very straightforward. Faster shutter speeds will result in clear pictures of motion while a slow shutter speed will make it blurry.

WHAT'S APPARENT ABOUT APERTURE

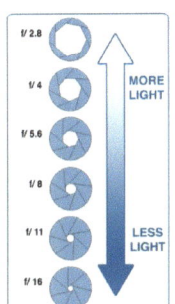

FIGURE 2. APERTURE MEASUREMENTS

If an aperture is to be explained in simple terms, then it is how you can control the size of the camera's lens. The larger an aperture is, the more light it will let into the camera. While this may have been simple to understand, grasping how aperture's size is measured is a bit tricky. This is because it is measured in f-stops. The higher the f-stop values, the lower the amount of light that will be let into the camera. Thus, a lower f-stop value such as f/22 will let in a small amount of light as compared to an aperture set at f/2.8. How can you use this information to take better pictures? Well, the f-stop values influence exposure. So, if you want a brighter photo, you can let more light in by increasing the f-stop value. This nifty trick will come in handy in situations where there is less light and pictures come out dark. The reverse is true for when you are shooting outside on a sunny day.

UNCOVERING THE INTERNATIONAL STANDARDS ORGANIZATION (ISO)

You and the ISO button on your camera may be unacquainted for now but that will soon change! The ISO can clue you in when it comes to your camera's sensitivity to light. With a higher ISO, you won't need a flash to capture images in places with low light. However, increasing the ISO will also increase the amount of noise within the photograph. Thus, a photograph that has been taken with an ISO value of 100 will be much sharper than say one where the ISO was 4000. How can you make the ISO work for you, if it also makes pictures grainier? The first thing you need to keep in mind is that the noise will start to appear at ISO values higher than 400, depending on the camera type. The next thing for you to remember is that at times, you will have to settle for a grainy photograph, if you want to avoid using the flash. For best results, use the guide given below to take good pictures:

- If you are outside in the sun, then keep the ISO value on 100
- If you are indoors in a dark room, then the ISO value could be as high as 1600 or even higher
- For overcast environments and open shade, a value of 400 ISO will do just fine
- You might have to increase the value to more than 600, if you are taking a picture late in the evening
- The ISO value would have to be as high as 800 and higher, if you are taking pictures inside with average lighting

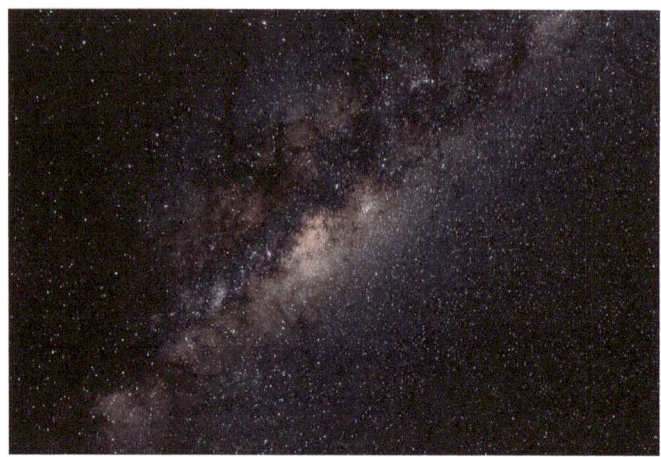

FIGURE 3. TAKEN WITH ISO 800

Together, the shutter speed, aperture, and ISO form the exposure triangle. If you are still unclear as to how they work in combination, try wrapping your head around this metaphor. If you think of your camera as having a window that might be used to look outside, then the shutter will be the parts that open and close it. In turn, how long the shutter stays open will determine the shutter speed. That means, if you want to let in more light through the window, the shutters will have to stay open for longer. Now, let us try to fit the aperture in this metaphor. While the shutter is letting light in, the aperture is the size of the window itself. Consequently, the bigger the window, the brighter the room it looks into will be. Lastly, the ISO can be included in this analogy by imagining that you stand inside the room, wearing shades. Even if more light is let into the room, your eyes will be unable to feel its intensity. Think of that as your camera being at a low ISO setting.

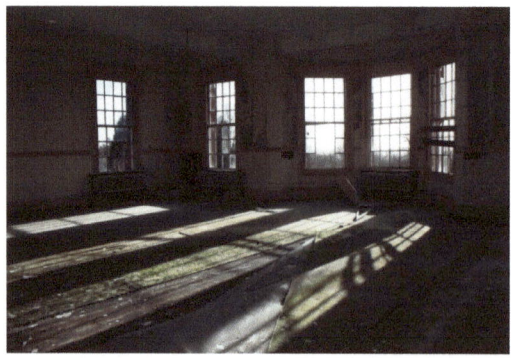

FIGURE 4. IT IS ALL ABOUT LETTING THE LIGHT IN

Now, with the example above, it is easy to see that there is no single way to increase how much light will enter your camera. You can increase the amount of light by leaving the shutters open for a longer time at low shutter speed. The same effect might be achieved with an increase in the size of the aperture. Similarly, larger ISO values will do the same thing i.e. let more light into the camera so that the pictures will be brighter, if a little grainier. Still confused? Don't worry, ryancranephotography.com will make exposure triangle even more easier for you to understand!

The Art of Proper Composition

If your pictures are coming out dull, then it might be connected to how well you have set the scene. You know it can't be the subject because it is fantastic. It means the poor photo composition is to blame! In fact, a well-set scene may even make the most everyday situations come out magical. If you have been looking for some tips on how to improve the photo composition of your pictures, then look no further. With these tips, you will be easily able to transform your images.

While these tips will work for you, it would not do to take them as rules. Don't try to remember all of them every time you are taking a picture. As with most skills, the more you practice, the more natural they will become and you won't even have to make a conscious effort to apply them. Practicing will help you see which tip will be the right choice for a given situation.

Rule of Thirds

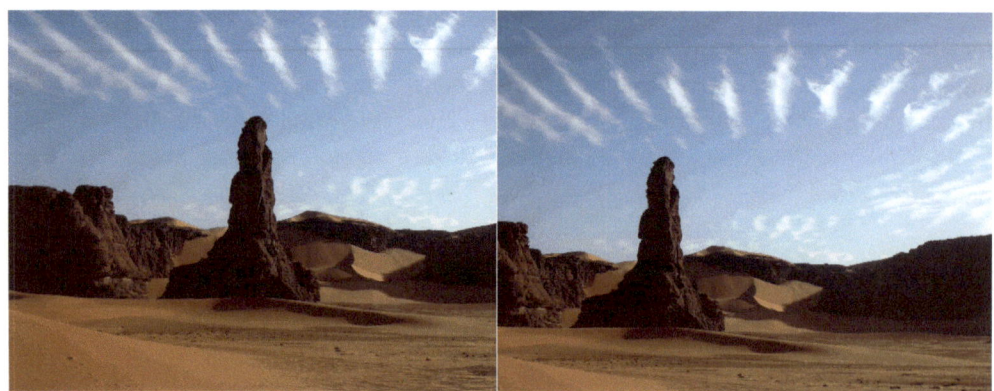

FIGURE 5 PRACTICING THE RULE

In order to make use of this one, you will need to see the image you are about to take as having 9 equal segments. Imagine that the segments have been divided by two horizontal and as many vertical lines. Now that you can visualize it in your mind, try to place the important parts of the picture where the points intersect. This will make the picture come out more balanced.

The Golden Ratio

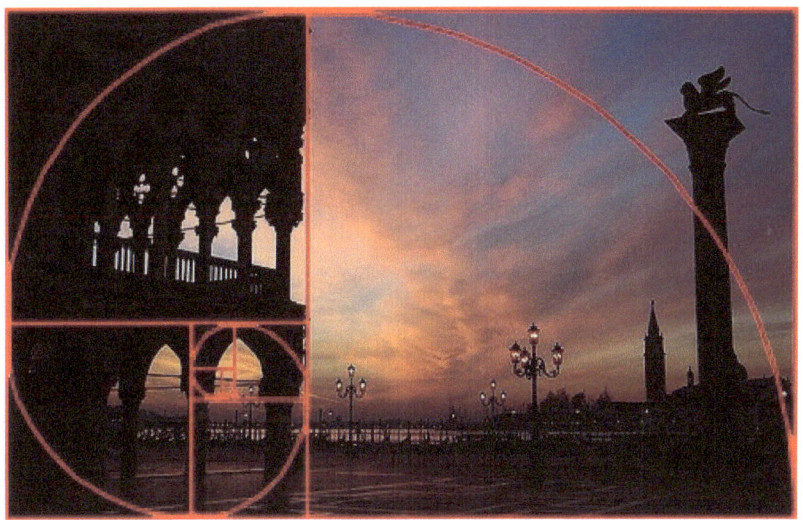

FIGURE 6. GOLDEN RATIO

The golden ratio might sound confusing but it really isn't. Just as you used the first rule to divide your picture into thirds, you will have to do some visualizing for this one as well. This time, the scene is to be seen as divided into 1: 1.618 sections. In easy words, close to 3/8ths of the lines will fall in the upper and lower parts of the frame. This will leave 2/8ths of the lines that will be concentrated in the centre. Many classical works of art have been designed by using the golden ratio, difficult as it may be to understand.

HORIZON LINE PLACEMENT

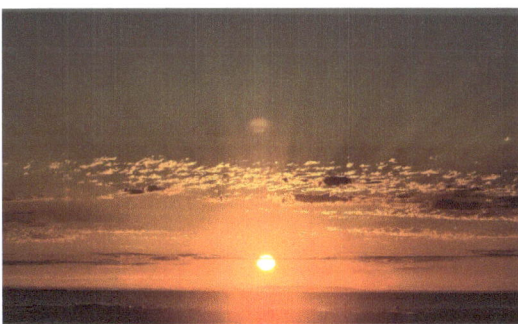

Except for when you are shooting a reflection, the best arrangement for the placement of the horizon line is above or below the middle of the frame. If you have been taking pictures where the horizon line falls right in the center of the image, then that might need to change. When shooting a reflection shot, you can follow your old approach and keep the horizon in the center of the image. This will result in equal division of the elements between the upper and lower parts of the scene surrounding the reflection. If for instance, you were taking a picture of a landscape, then placing the horizon line nearer to the top would work. Alternatively, you can also try placing it closer to the bottom and see if that works better.

LEAVE OUT THE REST

For the perfect photo composition, there is one important decision that you will need to make every time. Think which of the elements you will be including within the shot and which you will be leaving out. This is necessary in terms of deciding how well the elements that make the cut relate to each other. If they don't jive, then you will be better off taking them out. As far as composition is concerned, crowding a picture by filling it with multiple points of interest will not result in a good photograph. Instead, be selective and leave out the rest and you might end up with a photograph that is dramatic but simply composed.

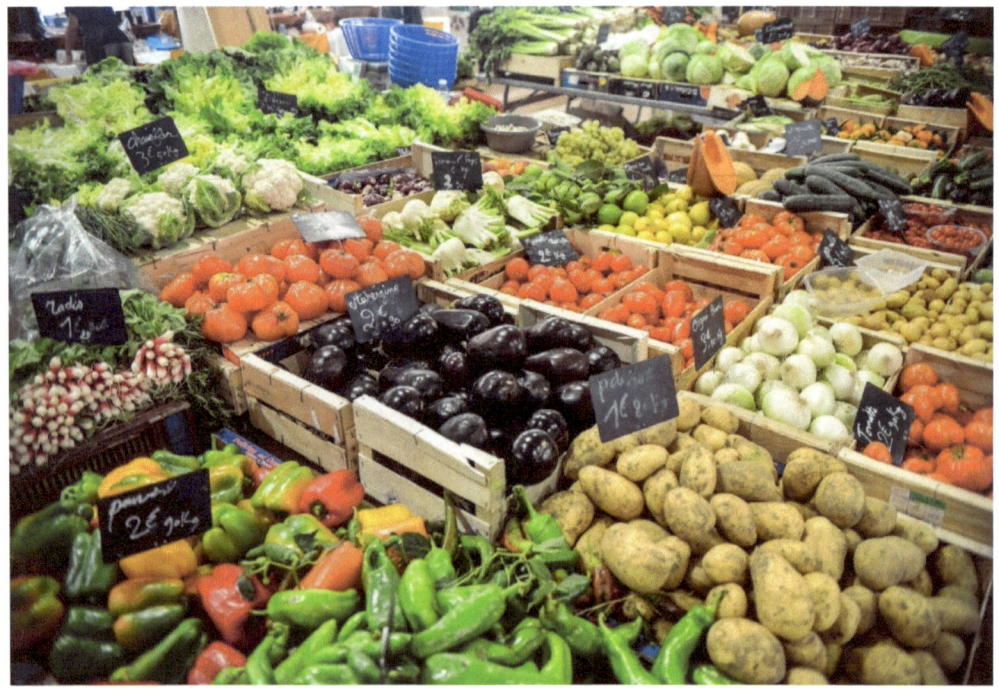

FIGURE 7. TOO MANY ELEMENTS

BALANCE MATTERS

While following the rule of thirds may work in some situations, it won't be the right choice for every photograph. At times, following that rule could end in an interesting but emptier-looking photo. Thus, if you think that the weight of your subject is not matching the weight of other objects within a scene, then you will need to add in other things to fill the space.

OTHER SHAPES

Just as the rule of thirds won't work every time, so would the golden ratio. If your image contains diagonals, then you would be better off with a golden triangle. In order to make use of this technique, you will have to split the image diagonally. The next thing you need to do is draw a line extending from one corner in a way that it meets the first diagonal line at a right angle. The objects that are part of your photograph should thus be falling inside the triangles that you just made.

RULING THE ODD ONE OUT

One of the simpler ideas, this technique resembles the rule of thirds. It is thought that images containing an odd number of elements are more pleasing to the eye than ones with an even number of things. When we look at an image, our eyes tend to gravitate towards the middle, if it features a group of subjects. That means, if your picture ends up with a void in it right in the centre, then that is where your viewer's eye will travel.

NOT ADHERING TO THE PREVIOUS RULE

It has been mentioned before that you should not adhere to the rules mentioned here. In fact, it is best to consider them as guides and try fitting the right one into each picture you take. That means, there will be photographs where you will need to leave some space. In order to make that happen in the right way, think of your frame as a box. Now that you have a box, you will be filling it with your subject. Now, you don't want to overstuff the box or it will overflow. Therefore, sometimes you will need a bigger box so that your subject has some space to move. This will be necessary if you are photographing a subject who is in motion. There are pictures where the subject is looking at something on/off-camera. If that is the case, then leaving some white space i.e. part of the frame where nothing is happening, will make for a better photograph.

For more tips and tricks, check out http://improveyourphotographyonline.com/

Making Manual Mode Less Back-Breaking

The question that is probably swirling in your mind after having read the chapter's name is why shoot in manual mode anyway. The answer is quite simply that when you shoot in manual mode, you will have complete control over everything that is going in the picture. In order to completely master the manual mode, you will need to become an expert at combining the three elements of the exposure triangle i.e. ISO, aperture, and shutter speed. While each of the individual elements has been covered in a previous chapter, we will still touch on them again in this one. Along with that, here are some situations where being adept at shooting in the manual mode will be an advantage:

- If you are planning to take a photograph that is a silhouette
- In cases where you want to end up with a Bokeh. These photographs are a combination of circles of light on a blurred background.

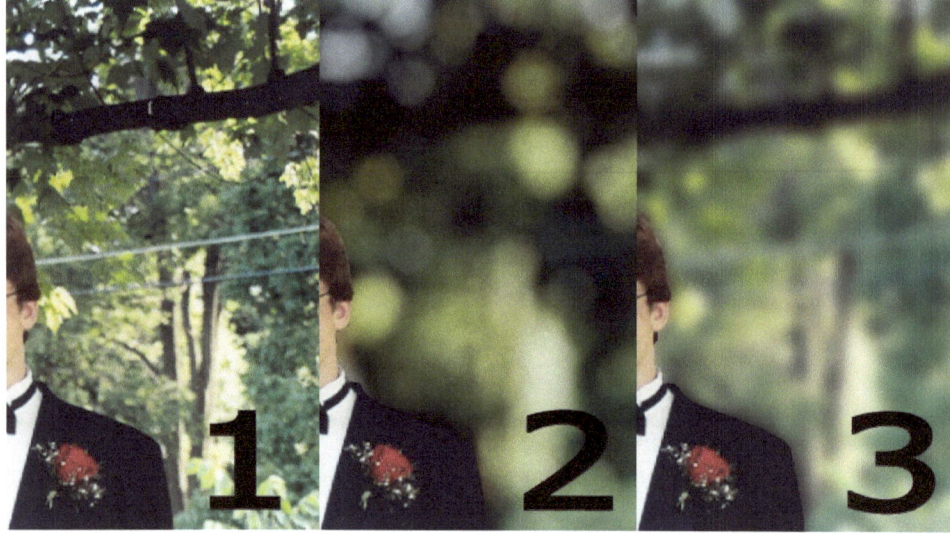

- In order to take a picture that will need a creative shot, focal point, or an angle to come out perfectly
- When you are shooting in low light, then knowing how to operate the manual mode will prevent unexpected flash from ruining your pictures
- If you want a picture that makes use of artistic blur to represent motion

One of the biggest drawbacks is that is associated with shooting in manual mode is that it is a time consuming process. Since you have to specify each setting by hand, it will take you much longer to take a picture in manual mode, even if all the settings are under your complete control. If you are to be the best at your craft, then you will have to balance the pros and cons of shooting in each mode for every shoot. Know when it will be the right choice to take your time and get every detail right by shooting in manual mode and when it is okay to rely on preset modes.

ISO

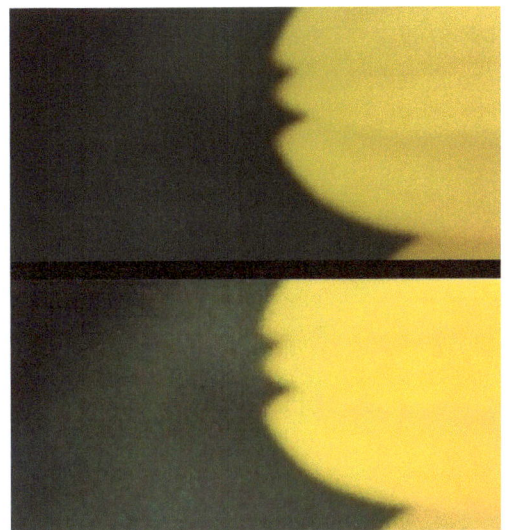

As you have already read and probably knew before that, ISO refers to how sensitivity your camera's sensor is to light. That means, if you are shooting outside on a bright sunny day, then the ISO setting in your camera should be as low as 100. If it is a cloudy day, then your sensor will need to be exposed to more light and the ISO setting will need to be increased slightly. For situations where you are shooting indoors or are in a darker place, then the ISO setting might have to be as high as 800-1600. The same goes for any shoots that take place at night. Remember that with high ISO settings, the pictures will come out grainier.

APERTURE

As mentioned before, the aperture is the lens's diaphragm's opening and its settings work backward. The higher settings for the aperture will mean a smaller number and vice versa. The range of distance at which the subject in the photograph appears sharp is known as the Depth of Field. The aperture of your lens determines the Depth of Field.

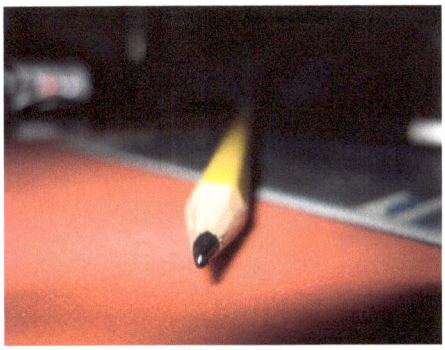

FIGURE 8. SHALLOW DEPTH OF FIELD

If the value of the aperture has you consider, try to keep this simple example in mind: if the aperture setting is small, then the subject you've focused on will be sharp. This is because a smaller number means a larger aperture. If you want to focus on the subject, as well as, the things in the background, then choosing a small number won't work. A large number meaning a small aperture would make all the elements of the picture sharp, regardless of their distance.

The aperture values are measured in f/stop values. If the f/stop value is small, then a large part of the lens has been opened. What this means is that more light will be entering the lens and falling on the sensor. Consequently, the background will be blurry due to less depth of field. The opposite is true for higher f/stop values.

Shutter Speed

The last setting that you need to know how to handle happens to be the shutter speed of your camera. The simplest way of describing shutter speed is the duration for which your camera's shutter will stay open. If the shutter stays open for longer, then the camera sensor will be exposed to light for a longer time. A longer exposure time can mean you will be able to photograph the stars with your camera, and blur people and waterfalls. Yet another use of long exposure time is that it comes in handy when you are shooting in low light.

Conversely, with an exposure as short as say 1/5000, capturing of an object on the move becomes possible. That means, you can photograph a cyclist who passes by and yet end up with a clear, sharp picture. If you are shooting outside on a sunny day, then you can also use a short exposure to take pictures that require large aperture.

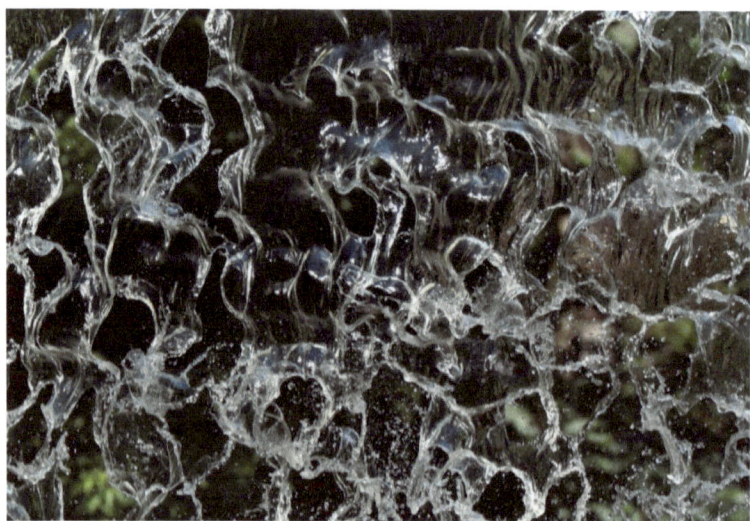

FIGURE 9. YOU WILL NEED A QUICK SHUTTER SPEED TO CAPTURE THE WATER'S MOVEMENT IN A WATERFALL

The one caveat that comes from a short exposure time or faster shutter speed is related to you and not your camera! The smaller the time of exposure, the more likely that your camera will be recording the movement your hands make. In order to avoid that, you can use a tripod. For a good picture, you should try to support yourself against a wall and stop breathing for a second or two. The next thing is to make sure that your face is not touching the viewer before pressing the shutter.

COMBINING THE SETTINGS

When you shoot in manual mode, as its name suggests, you have to set everything yourself. While this gives you complete control over the photograph, it also means that the settings of your choice complement each other. Try to visualize the combined effect of the trinity of the exposure triangle before taking a photograph. One way of lessening the confusion that is likely to result from trying to manage all three things at once is to prioritize. Think which of the three is the most important and spend some time getting that element right. Think if you'd rather focus on getting a shallow depth of field or the right light. If you choose the former, then you need to pay attention to the camera's aperture. The ISO should be your priority for the latter. On the other hand, if you want to capture a subject in motion and/or avoid motion blur, then you will need to concentrate on shutter speed. Thus, it depends upon your objective.

The lower part of most cameras will include a little meter that lets you know whether you are over- or under-exposed when shooting in manual mode. Your goal should be to avoid both extremes and get the pointer to stay in the centre.

Sometimes Raw is Better

What is RAW?

Let us start with a brief description of what the RAW file that your camera creates is. More importantly, what can you do with such a file? A RAW file is the unedited and unchanged file that is sent to your memory card by the camera sensor. While they may have become obsolete now, the RAW file is actually the negatives on the film that we needed to get developed before using them.

Your camera makes irreversible changes to the photograph that you take in the form of jpeg files. Thus, you will be getting the product after it has been developed. Of course, this will be time saving; however, it will also mean that you won't have the freedom to edit the jpeg files if you are not satisfied with how they have come out. We say that because with every edit you make on the photograph, its quality suffers. The reason behind the degradation of the quality is that editing is the result of change in the photograph's pixels. If you were making these edits on a RAW file, you won't be manipulating the pixels. Instead, it is as if you add extra layers to the original picture, which is why the quality remains unaffected.

Where To Shoot RAW?

If you want to get a RAW file of a photograph, then you will have to forego the auto mode. It is only possible to end up with RAW, if you are shooting in manual or semi-manual mode. When you shoot in auto mode, the result will be jpeg.

Why Not Raw?

Something to keep in mind when you aim to get the RAW images is if you have the software that can read them correctly. Older versions of the software might not be compatible with the new camera's RAW files and you won't be able to edit them. Additionally, there may also be a problem with the format of the RAW files. If the image is in jpeg, then you don't have to worry. Due to there not being a standard RAW file extension, its format will often depend on the camera manufacturers.

Before shooting in manual mode and thinking about editing the resulting RAW files, ensure that you the right version of the software you will need. If you are updating the software, then check compatibility. The software needs to be compatible with your camera's raw file format.

Why RAW?

Since RAW files have much more detailed information, you can edit your photograph more thoroughly. In fact, the amount of information contained in such a file could mean it is even possible to change some of your cameras settings after taking the photo and uploading it to your computer. Some of the amendments that you can make include the exposure setting, white balance etc. When you are done with the editing, all you need to do is convert the RAW file into a format of your preference, such as TIFF or JPEG.

How about RAW + JPEG?

If you don't want to risk losing your photos, then you might want to take this route and shoot in both RAW + JPEG. While this may be the safest route, you will also have to dedicate considerably large space to save the pictures on your memory card /hard drive etc.

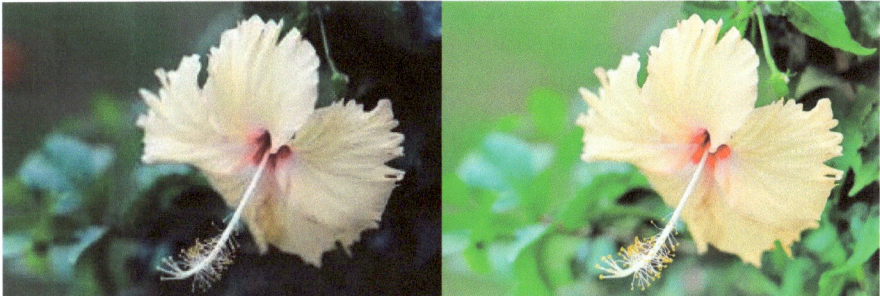

If you do intend to follow this tip, then you might want to keep one other thing in mind. While shooting in both forms side to side, the jpeg shots will be looking better as compared to the RAW ones. Do not worry if that is so since the JPEG is the result of minor adjustments made by your camera before it compresses your photo. On the other hand, the raw file comes off looking duller than its counterpart looks. Nevertheless, it will also have more potential for improvements without quality compromises.

Think of the improvements you make on a RAW file as sticking a post-it note on a piece of paper. When you want to revert to the original or change something else, all you need to do is remove the post-it. All the editing you want without any of the pixels being broken.

Which Types of RAW?

As mentioned before, there is no universal RAW format that is followed by all brands. That means, the format your camera uses will depend on its manufacturers. For instance, Canon cameras when shooting in RAW produce a .CR2 file. Similarly, Nikon cameras will save a .NEF file. The extension will be different for Kodak, Sony, Pentax, and Olympus, as well.

RAW vs. JPEG

Summarized here are some of the advantages that shooting in RAW has over the JPEG mode:

Advantages

- Editing in RAW mode does not compromise the picture's quality. This non-destructive editing is possible because the amendments are being stuck on the file and not influencing the pixels like it does in jpeg.

- When you save a picture as a RAW file, you also save all the information that comes with it. That means fixing areas of the picture that either are under- or overexposed becomes easier. If you think the photograph has lost some of the pertinent detail while it was converted to jpeg, then you can bring it back with a RAW file.

- Trying to make an image appear sharper when it is saved in jpeg format can result in a low quality photograph. The RAW format is your best choice if you also want to retain the ability to sharpen the image during post-processing.

- Noise reduction is possible with RAW files to a certain extent. Doing the same thing on a jpeg file often results in the loss of a lot of detail.

- Have your camera work to its fullest potential when you shoot in RAW. This is because each file is saved with all of the data that your camera's sensor senses and sends to storage. There is less chance of the picture losing some of its detail as compared to when it is converted to JPEG format.

- It is easy to fix white balance in RAW according to your needs and mood as opposed to in JPEG where it will remain unchanged.

- When you save a photograph in jpg format, then converting it to RGB for use on the web or CMYK for print could mean loss of quality. This is not the case with RAW files, which can be optimized for both web and print.

- An HDR picture is actually made of three pictures: one is underexposed, the other is overexposed, and the third one is a well exposed image. The purpose of using different modes of exposure is to get the details from the dark and lighter parts of the scene that is being photographed. As evident, the smallest details tend to matter when it comes to HDR. If you use different jpeg files for HDR editing, the result will likely be of low quality. This won't be the case with RAW files.

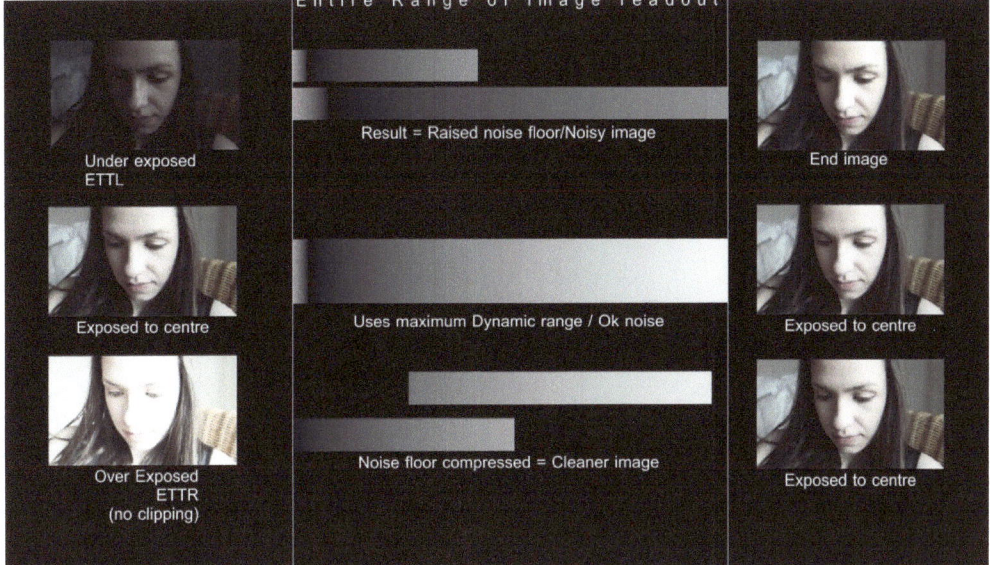

Under exposed
ETTL

Exposed to centre

Over Exposed
ETTR
(no clipping)

Result = Raised noise floor/Noisy image

Uses maximum Dynamic range / Ok noise

Noise floor compressed = Cleaner image

End image

Exposed to centre

Exposed to centre

DISADVANTAGES

- RAW files are not sharing friendly since they will need to be processed before you can share them.

- RAW files will take much more space on your memory card or hard disk since they are bigger in size as compared to the JPEG.

- It takes time to process and convert the RAW files and if you are short on time, then this won't be the right choice for you.

- Moreover, since the files are larger, it will take the camera more time to write the images to the memory card, thus slowing down during the process.

FINAL VERDICT

The cons may make you think that RAW files are not worth the hassle. However, that would be a mistake! You can find a solution to all the cons that were mentioned above. If the files are too big, then you can invest in a memory card that not only has more storage space but also works faster. If processing each photo takes a lot of time that you'd rather spend sharing them, then there is a solution for that too. If you shoot in both jpeg and RAW, then you can start sharing right away. You will be sharing the images that come out good in jpeg anyway, so go ahead and do so. The images that you think will require improvement can be edited in the RAW mode before you share them.

THE RIGHT WAY TO BEGIN PHOTOGRAPHY

KNOW THY CAMERA

METERING MODES

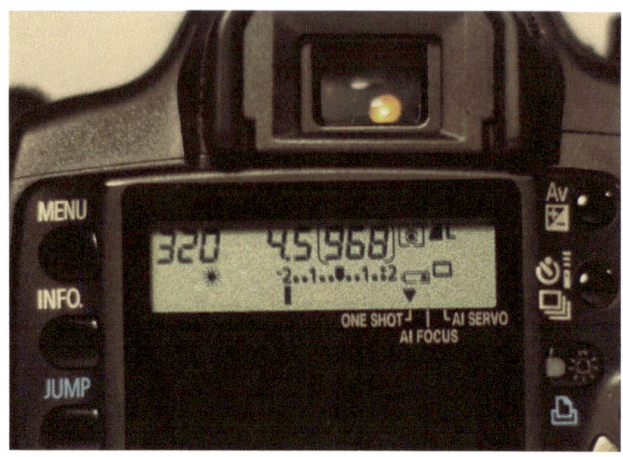

While the exposure triangle is usually simplified into a combination of three elements i.e. ISO, aperture, and shutter speed, it isn't as easy as that. In order to be a good photographer, you will need to do some reading on exposure. Moreover, how your camera looks at light is also important. There are also various metering modes on your camera that tell it how to look at a scene and you will have to decide which mode suits best. A picture that has been taken using the evaluative mode will drastically differ from one that was captured in the spot metering. If you do not get the exposure right, then your pictures might come out under- or overexposed!

SHOOTING MODES

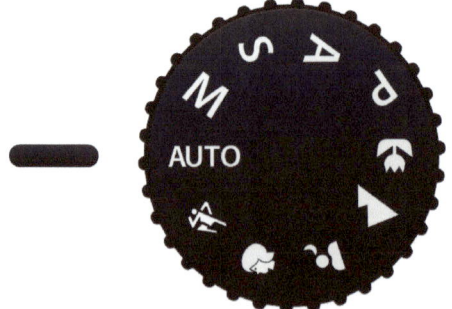

So many different types of modes exist that it can be difficult to know them all. However, in order to get better at taking pictures, you will need to read up on them. There is the auto mode, and then there is also the pre-programmed option. Cameras will also have an Aperture or Shutter Speed Priority and you can choose between them, depending on your needs. There are many misconceptions floating out there about which modes are best under which conditions. Moreover, many people will also swear by auto mode since manual mode seems like too much work to them. However, there are conditions when only the manual mode will work. Thus, you need to do some reading and practicing with each mode to find out which mode will serve you better in a particular shoot.

HISTOGRAMS

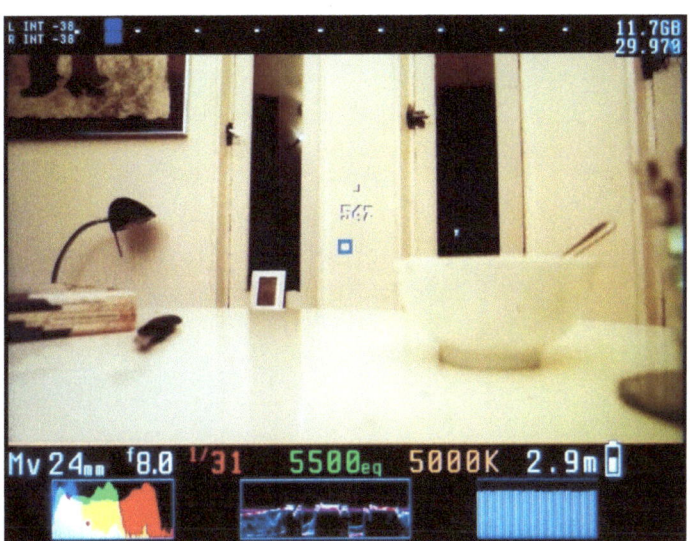

One of the most powerful and yet underutilized tool, the histogram can be quite useful of you know how to use it. Its purpose is to show you an exposure in a mathematical light after you have taken the photo. Simply put, histograms will tell you the degree of evenness of the exposure of a photo. Do not depend on an LCD screen to perform this function for you. This is because the ambient lighting conditions can influence not only the photograph but also the LCD screen itself. That is why you cannot depend on LCDs and should know how to make the best use of histograms.

GETTING BETTER AT IT

That is easy for us to say, you think, but how am I supposed to become a good photographer when there are so many misconceptions to clear and things to learn. Don't worry, here are some ways you can do just that:

LET THE PROS HELP

One way to get better at this craft is to look for photography clubs that meet in your area. It is highly likely that you will come across more than one of them. If you are on a tight budget, then look for clubs that are free and enroll in one. Not only will you be learning from your fellow photographers when you join one of those clubs, there will be other advantages. Once you become a part of that community, it is likely you will also be given information about events that you can attend and photograph.

Another way to learn is to look up advanced photographers. If you find one who is locally situated, then you can always request them to let you assist them. As you work a job with them, you will learn more about expert tips and techniques that only a pro like them can offer!

LANDSCAPE PHOTOGRAPHY PLAYS BY DIFFERENT RULES

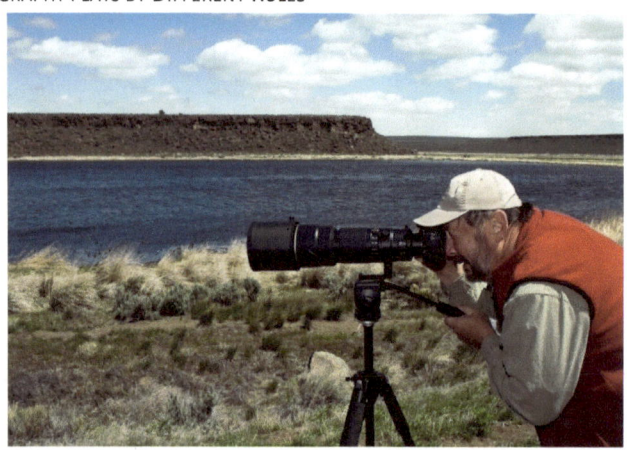

If you are interested in landscape photography, then learning how to use a circular polarizer might be a good idea. While you should always try shooting with what you own, instead of spending a lot of money on gadgets. However, in this case, you should make an exception. A polarizer is a very useful gadget for a photographer.

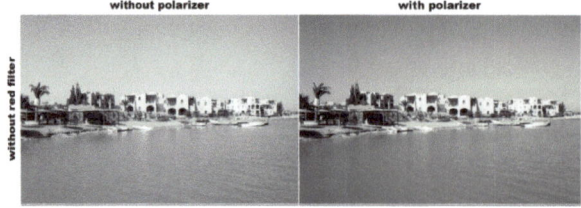

TRIPOD CAN COME IN HANDY

You should get a tripod if you don't already own one. A tripod could create new opportunities for you and help you experiment more. With it, you can try new things with low light photography, such as shooting at night. It can make for some beautiful images. With a tripod, you can

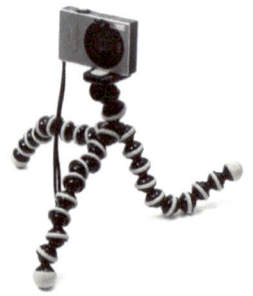

also capture interesting pictures of both moving and non-moving subjects. Use it to take sharp pictures of non-moving subjects while blurring out moving ones.

TIMING ISN'T JUST CRUCIAL FOR JOKES

If you are going to shoot during different times of the day, then it is best to pick the right hour to do it. If you are shooting in bright sunlight, then it is likely that you will end up with bad photographs. This is because it can produce ugly shadows on and around the subjects. Therefore, if you must shoot in the morning, then try to do so early in the morning. Similarly, late in the afternoon, the light will be softer and make for good pictures. In order to catch a sunrise and sunset at the right time, you can always Google the time and be there on time.

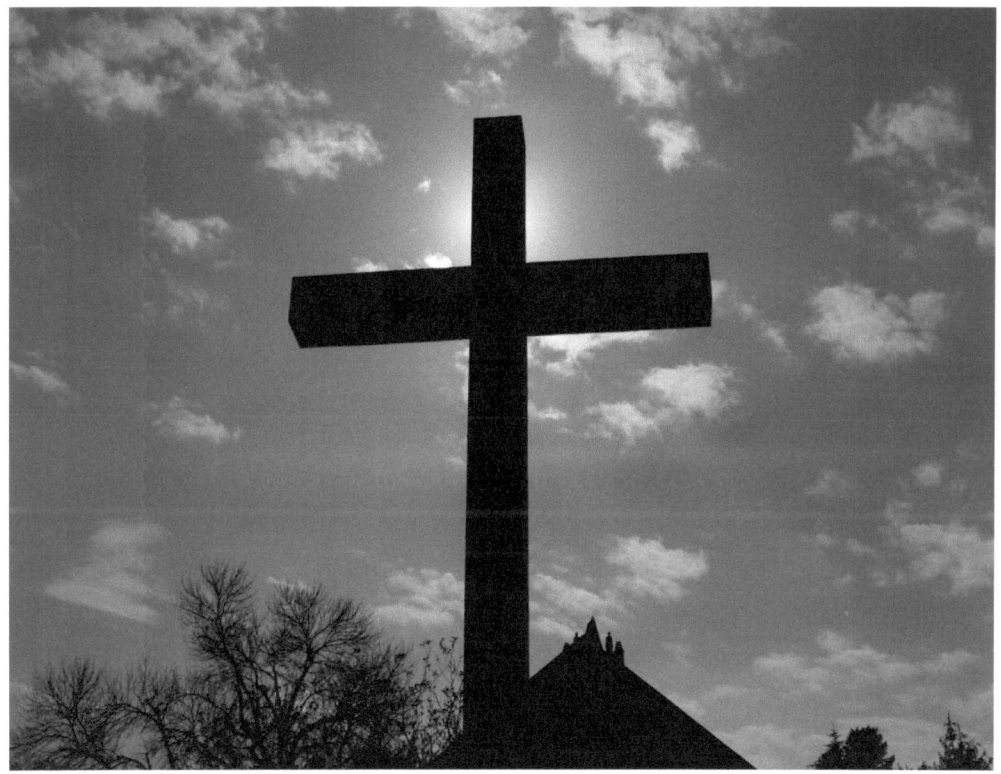

FIGURE 10 DIFFUSED LIGHT

The next thing you need to take into consideration are the weather conditions. Since clouds can make the light diffused, a cloudy day is perfect for shooting portraits. However, if the cloud cover is too thick and dense, it will be too dark for photography. It will be especially difficult to shoot fast-moving objects in such an environment. You will have to try and see what works for you and use that in your pictures.

This is a topic that will be covered in detail in one of our later books but the time for storing your pictures manually on your hard drive is long past. You need to start using the amazingly easy to use tool or Adobe Photoshop Lightroom. Without it, you might be using Adobe Photoshop + Camera Raw to process your images. The problem with doing that is that the whole process painstakingly long and difficult. There is also the added complication of files scattered among the various folders when you use the conventional method. Once you switch to Lightroom, you will be able to store, process and organize your pictures in a much more efficient way. Moreover, Camera Raw – Lightroom has all the features that are found in Camera Raw.

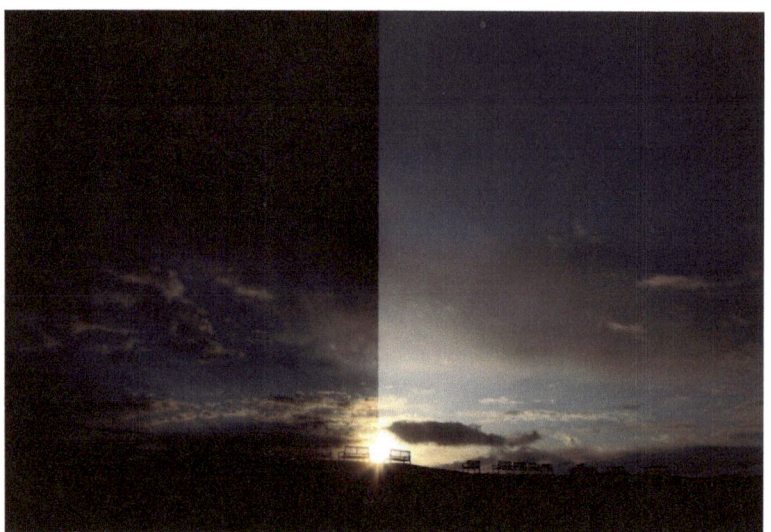

FIGURE 11. BEFORE AND AFTER POST-PROCESSING

Want Pictures, Must Travel

If you want to take great pictures, then you can't just sit at home and wait for the opportunities to come walking. Instead, you are the one who will have to do some walking! Some good places that will make for excellent pictures include local, state, and national parks. Try to pick ones that are within driving distance because nobody expects you to travel overseas just for a picture. Visit such a place and spend some time looking around for a place that would potentially make a good subject.

If you are interested in landscape photography, then you will need some practice to figure out what works and what doesn't. For example, if you come across a still lake, you can use it to photograph an image where its surface mirrors the trees in the background etc. In order for a spectacular image though, you might have to go to the lake at sunrise and sunset. It is highly possible that you will only be able to get the image that you are satisfied with after more than one visit.

If on the other hand, you are into portrait photography, then what you will need is a good background. The good news is that it is often easy to find a good background. It only needs to be something interesting and you will need to use your imagination for that. It could be a painted fence, an old tree, or a building.

Special Conditions Require Special Treatment

Underwater

First Things First

This may seem like the most obvious tip but we will mention it anyway. In order to be a good at underwater photography, you need to start with the foundation. That means, you need to know how to swim and must possess uber water skills. If you do not know how to stay buoyant, how do you expect to take pictures that are well composed and well- lit? It isn't just the quality of the pictures that might suffer. If you keep crashing into the reef while trying to take your shots, you will also be causing harm to the environment. Lastly, it is very important that you have knowledge of decompression sickness. Since it is easy to lose track of time during underwater photography, you can easily forget that you have a limited air supply to depend upon. In order to be a good photographer while underwater, you will need to be an adept diver and swimmer.

Shedding a Light

While you can engage in underwater photography during all times of the day, there is one slot when the pictures will turn out perfect. A bright afternoon is such a time since that is when sunlight is in abundance and travels deep into the water. However, you may not always have

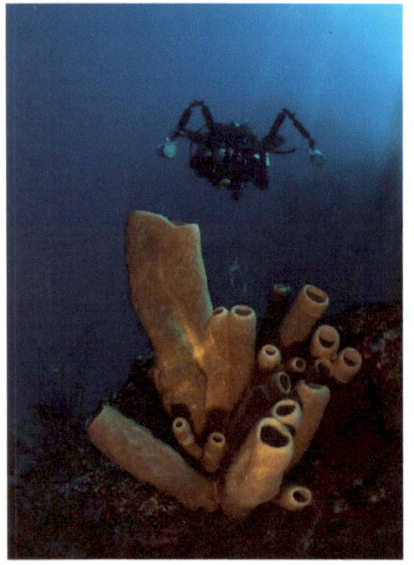

the freedom to pick that time for all your shoots. If you must take images while swimming in gloomy waters or are too deep for sunlight to make much of a difference, artificial light or flash can get rid of the shadows. Using such a light source will also help bring out the beautiful colors that are found underwater. In case your camera does not have a flash that is strong enough or there is no built-in flash, you can always rent an external one. Using an underwater strobe is yet another alternative. If you are using an external flash, it may make the particles between you and the subject light up, causing white spots to appear in the image. To avoid what is called backscatter, have the external flash placed at an angle towards the lens.

FIGURE 12. STROBES POSITIONED TO AVOID BACKSCATTER

Food

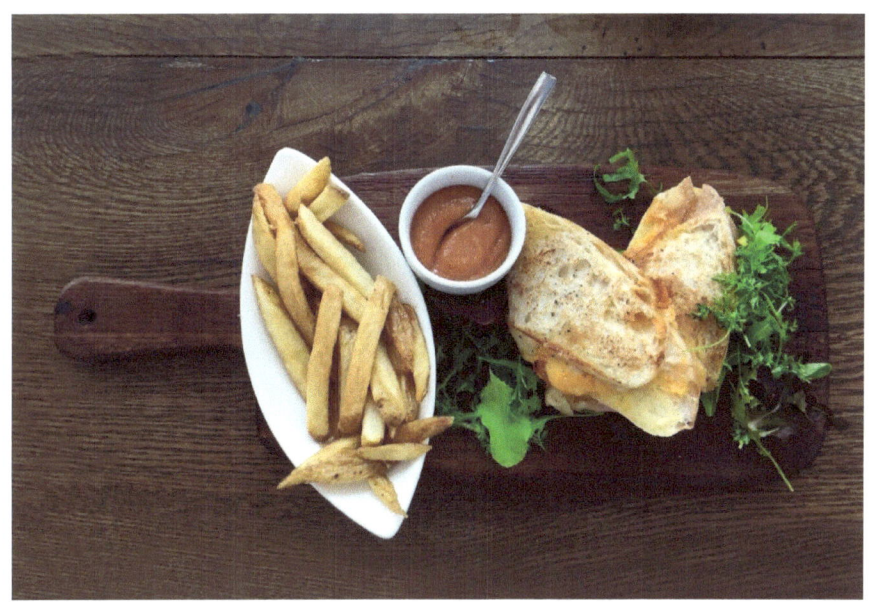

INGREDIENTS CAN MAKE OR BREAK A SHOOT

The dish that you are going to be photographing is scrumptious. You know it and the chef knows it. However, your viewer is not going to taste it. They will only have your image to go by and it needs to be convincing enough. In that vein, if you include potatoes that are heavenly crispy but looked wrinkled; you would have lost the viewer. Either replace the damaged ingredients or pick one that isn't!

WISE CHOICE OF PLATE IS AS IMPORTANT AS WISE CHOICE OF PALETTE

If it is important for an image to have the right ingredients, then it is equally important that you use the right medium to show them off! We mean, of course, the plate or bowl that you will be putting the food in. It needs to be as spectacular or all the hard work will go to waste. While an unconventional shape, such as a rectangular plate might look delightfully quirky, it is also more likely to wind up looking wonky. It will be harder to shoot most shapes as compared to shooting the average round shaped plate. What can you do to keep things fresh, if you can't change the shape of the plate? Change the size and switch to a salad-size plate. Pick a plate with an eye catching pattern or a bright color to add some character to the image.

THE RIGHT BACKGROUND MAKES THE RIGHT PICTURE

Now that you have the freshest ingredients making your images beautiful and the right plate to showcase them, the next thing you need to focus on is the background. Try to take a step away from what you have already used in previous shoots. The cutting board may look amazing but you may have used it one times too many. If you want to shake things up, use a cutting board that is another color than the boring old brown. Why not paint over the old one? In fact, why not use the countertop as the background? Or a tablecloth?

FOOD PHOTOGRAPHY REQUIRES PERSONALITY

If you are going to excel at food photography, then your pictures need to be multi-dimensional. One way to get that going for you is by addition of things that will make the images more engaging. You can add placements, such as napkins, utensils etc to do that. However, when you are bringing other elements in to the picture, think very carefully in terms of color. If you are unsure about your choice of colors, then you can use a color wheel. It will make it easier to pick accessories that are in colors that complement each other.

GARDEN

THE RIGHT TIME

If you think that garden photography can only produce good results if the pictures are taken at a particular time, then you could not be more wrong! Almost anytime can be the right time for garden photography for one simple reason. At any given time, something is in bloom somewhere in the garden! If you are photographing your own garden, then you can also plant it accordingly. Try to be smart and choose the best plants for shade, which will be different from those that thrive in the sun. Once you get the idea, you can choose plants that will bring the colors that complement each other in your garden.

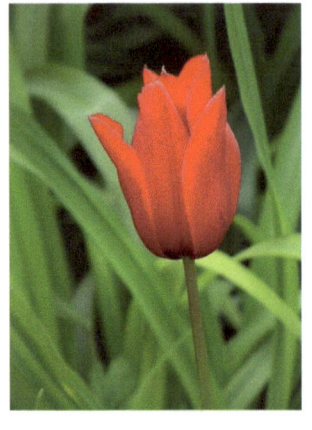

THE COLOR SCHEME

The colors that are within the frame of the photograph that you will be taking should agree with each other. That does not mean that you cannot use contrasting colors. What you need to ensure is that no matter what the color scheme is, it looks harmonious. You will achieve a completely different result if the garden design is based on contrasting colors. With contrast, comes an image rich with drama while colors that are similar toned will result in a picture that is both soft and romantic. Nevertheless, green happens to be the color that is almost always indispensible during a garden shoot. It is so important because it sets off everything else that will be included in the image. Think of a red colored flower plant against a green background and you will see how important green is.

NEVER STOP AT ONE

This tip will probably work for all kinds of photography. Instead of just taking a single shot, try to shoot multiple of them. With each shot, change a setting or the angle to end up with similar shots that are not the same. If you are using a digital camera, then you can easily check the results and take another series of photographs, if you don't like the first one.

PORTRAITS

CONNECT WITH THE SUBJECT

Make an effort and connect with your subject. The more comfortable they feel, the better the portrait is likely to come out. That could mean familiarizing yourself with what the subject is passionate about and then using it as a conversation starter. Another way to help them relax is by playing their favorite music playing. Make a point of talking to them beforehand and ask them about other details, such as their favorite article of clothing or color, preferable pose, and the purpose behind the portrait they have commissioned. Incorporating these elements or some of them within the shoot will go a long way in making them feel satisfied with the results.

EXPOSURE TRIANGLE ADVICE

For the best portraits, some of the following advice might come in handy. Remember that it won't work every time but can be used as a guideline. The aperture setting for most portraits should be between f/2.8-5.6. With this setting, the background will be slightly blurred due to a shallow depth of field while the subject will stand out better. Next, we move on to setting the right shutter speed for the portrait you will be shooting. Try to visualize that the focal length of the lens will also need to be factored in the decision or you will end up with a blurry picture. A good idea is to ensure that the focal length is lower than your shutter speed.

NEVER TAKE JUST ONE SHOT

When shooting portraits, it is always a good idea to switch your camera Into a continuous shooting mode. Instead of one picture, you will then end up with a series of images. This technique comes in handy when your subject is active within the picture or you are photographing kids. Once you are done, you can present the combination to the client, instead of just one static image.

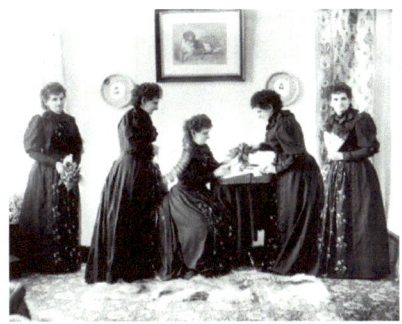

ABOUT THE AUTHOR

Ryan Crane is a well-known name in international published photography. Ryan developed his photography skills through painstakingly long hours of research and trial and error. Having carved a niche in the world, he now aims to help others who are just starting to step into the world of photographic art. Visit ryancranephotography.com to start learning today! Click improveyourphotographyonline.com, if you are a photographer looking to improve their craft.